The Art
of
Effective Delegation

ACTIONABLE TIPS AND TECHNIQUES
TO MAKE YOU A BETTER
SUPERVISOR, MANAGER, OR LEADER

Steven Howard

Caliente Press

The Art of Effective Delegation

Actionable Tips and Techniques
to Make You a Better
Supervisor, Manager, or Leader

ISBN: 978-1-943702-51-0 (print edition)
       978-1-943702-53-4 (Kindle edition)

Published by:
Caliente Press
1775 E Palm Canyon Drive, Suite 110-198
Palm Springs, CA 92264
www.CalientePress.com
Email: steven@CalientePress.com

Cover Design: Héctor Castañeda

Contents

Dedication

For Rodrigo S. Martineli

Client. Friend. Colleague.

*Together, we have developed
so many good people.*

*I admire your skills of delegation
and how you always balance
the pursuit of excellence
with the quality time you
spend with your family.*

*You are a shining example
of a Great Leader.*

Introduction To
The Art of Great Leadership Series

Welcome to *The Art of Great Leadership* series.

Having mentored, coached, and trained over 12,000 people over the past 30 years, I know that transitioning from a highly skilled and excellent Individual Contributor to a supervisor, manager, or team leader position can be quite challenging. There are many reasons for this, some of which will be highlighted below.

But first, the good news. You do not have to let the many transition traps that befall new leaders happen to you. With the right leadership education and coaching, you can be confidently prepared to handle these challenges and obstacles. *The Art of Great Leadership* series aims to put you squarely onto this path.

And, if you desire, you can become a great leader. A leader who is admired. A leader who is trusted. A leader capable of providing the motivation, coaching, feedback, development, and direction that your team members want and need.

Great leadership is an art. It is the art of achieving progress through the involvement and actions of others.

Here are four other things I believe about Great Leadership:

1. Leadership is about both people and results. If you must neglect one, reduce your focus on the results, for these will come when you have developed your people.

2. Great leaders are great listeners. They know they learn more from listening than from speaking.

3. Great leaders happen at all levels of organizations, not just in the executive suits or the ownership ranks.

4. People development is the single most important long-term priority and responsibility of all leaders at all levels of an organization. Great leaders ensure that this happens.

It is also possible to transition successfully from an Individual Contributor position into a new manager or supervisor role. Unfortunately, this is not a natural or easy transition. Research shows that over 60% of new supervisors and managers fail to transition effectively from individual contributors to new leadership roles.

Transitioning from a successful individual contributor role into a supervisory or manager position is fraught with challenges, concerns, and worries. This is a profound change that requires a new skill set to be successful. It also comes with high risks of failure, personal dissatisfaction, team disenchantment, and team member disengagement.

Why? Simply because too many first-time supervisors and managers are thrown into the deep end of the pool, with little guidance or direction and little or no formal training in leadership skills. They are expected to achieve results through others but often need more people motivation, engagement, feedback, and development skills.

They can also have tremendous difficulties communicating unpopular programs and decisions dictated from above and aligning team members with a newly formed strategic vision or change initiatives.

Complicating matters further, numerous pitfalls prevent excellent individual contributors from effectively transitioning into first-time supervisory and managerial responsibilities. Here are 12 transition traps that frequently derail new leaders, managers, and supervisors:

- ✓ Trying to accomplish too much too fast
- ✓ Wearing the "boss" hat too often, too soon
- ✓ Micromanaging due to fear of not knowing everything
- ✓ Trying to mandate buy-in rather than attaining it through influence leadership skills
- ✓ Believing you need to have all the answers
- ✓ Making changes too quickly and too soon
- ✓ Not understanding the priorities of their boss
- ✓ Not knowing their leadership philosophy
- ✓ Not thinking about their leadership mindset
- ✓ Failing to establish boundaries and expectations
- ✓ The inability to prioritize shifting projects, tasks, and deadlines
- ✓ Not knowing how to lead people through change

In *The Art of Great Leadership* book series and the companion *Art of Great Leadership* self-paced, online training program, I will help you overcome and avoid these transition traps.

The Art of Great Leadership collection is a practical, how-to series of informational books to help new and first-time managers and leaders excel in their newfound roles.

This series covers the major questions and concerns that supervisors, managers, and leaders have raised with me in conversations over the years. In each book, I will showcase best practices, tips, and techniques that have turned good managers into great leaders.

Topics we will cover in *The Art of Great Leadership* series include:

- Effective Feedback
- Motivation
- Employee Engagement
- Communicating as a Leader
- Conflict and Drama
- Relationship Building
- Foundations of Leadership
- Workplace Wellbeing
- Creating Cooperative Collaboration
- Transition Traps
- Developing People (and Self)

Please email me at steven@calienteleadership.com with other topics you would like to see included in *The Art of Great Leadership* series.

Here is something else I deeply believe. No leader, manager, or supervisor in today's world should wait around for their boss to tell them how to develop as a leader. It is time for individuals to stop waiting for your company to develop their leadership skills. Likewise, do not waste time on university programs or workshops full of theory but no practicality.

Be proactive. Start leading and controlling your own personal and professional development. To develop your leadership skills, seek leadership education, not a training program.

So, congratulations on being proactive by reading the editions of *The Art of Great Leadership* series that are most applicable to your needs and situation. If I can assist you on your journey, please contact me at steven@calienteleadership.com.

Great Leadership Defined

What is a leader?

In this book, a leader is defined as anyone who directly or indirectly leads people. Full stop.

This includes managers, supervisors, team leaders, first-line leaders, second-line leaders, and those higher in the organization. It also includes entrepreneurs, whether yours is a one-person business or a growing start-up.

I take the definition of a great leader to a higher echelon. I define Great Leadership as *the art of achieving progress through the involvement and actions of others*. Great leaders are strong in both leading people and leading for results, while good leaders typically excel at leading only one or the other.

In truth, everyone is a leader, if only to motivate and lead themselves. Thus, every Individual Contributor should consider themselves a leader as well. And each of you is capable of becoming a great leader.

The mindsets, skills, and behaviors in *The Art of Great Leadership* series will also serve you well in your personal life. Whether you are a parent, involved in community groups, or volunteering as a youth sports coach, applying and exhibiting the leadership skills, tips, and techniques found throughout *The Art of Great Leadership* series will help you in your endeavors.

Introduction

Delegation is important for leaders and their team members to grow.

Unfortunately, many first-time and First Line supervisors, team leaders, and managers often fear delegating. The question of "what if something goes wrong?" haunts their thinking about delegation.

That is a legitimate fear. And it links directly to the number one fear people have about delegating: if the person I delegate to screws up, it will be on me and make me look bad.

This often happens because leaders, managers, and supervisors have not been taught how to manage the delegation process. And it is a process.

This book will fix this lack of knowledge and understanding by providing you with a best-practice methodology for delegating and managing the delegation process. When you implement the tips and techniques in this book, you will no longer have to fear the negative consequences of delegating as you will have mastered them. Even better, you will free up time to tackle the more important aspects and duties of your role as a leader, including more time for developing people, strategizing, cognitive thinking, and problem-solving.

Leadership is an art. It is the art of achieving progress through the involvement and actions of others. One way to involve others is through delegation. Delegation is also critical for developing and growing the people reporting to you.

This makes delegation one of the most important tools you have as a leader. But to leverage this tool to the max, you have to develop your skills in using this tool. And, like any skill, you can learn, practice, enhance, and master the skill of delegation.

Delegation, like leadership, is also an art. There is no magic wand for delegation. There is no secret formula. And most importantly, delegation is not a tick-box activity where you send work over to someone, cross it off your to-do list, and then forget about it.

No, delegation is a dynamic process, meaning every delegated activity will differ from all others, even if only slightly. This is what makes managing the delegation process an art. And like any artist, you can (and will) get better at it by learning from each delegation experience.

Yes, delegation is a complex topic. But it need not be a complicated one. The tips and techniques – and most importantly, the delegation process detailed in this book – will reduce the complexity and complicatedness of delegation, especially for new managers, supervisors, and leaders.

I look forward to hearing how improving your skills in managing the delegation process powers your careers to greater heights.

Best wishes for continued success,
Steven Howard
September 2024

CHAPTER 1

What Is Delegating?

Before you read this chapter, I encourage you to pause and answer these two questions:

a) How would you define delegation?

b) Why is delegation beneficial to you as a supervisor, manager, or leader?

The answer to the question on the definition of delegation is straightforward:

*Delegation is the transfer of a task, assignment, project, or duty **that the manager usually performs** from the manager to someone else (usually a direct report).*

As the bold type indicates, delegation is different from assigning work, tasks, jobs, or projects to someone on your team because delegation involves things you are usually performing.

Here is the difference.

A new task is required to be performed and accomplished by your team. As the team manager, you evaluate the task and assess the skills and time capacity availability of your team members. You decide that Susan is most suited to handle this task and has the time available to complete it within the stipulated timeframe.

This scenario is assigning work. It is not delegation since the task is not something that you, as the manager of the team, would normally do.

Now let's look at another scenario. Serena is a manager of a department and she writes the monthly department newsletter. She has done it since taking over the department many months ago. But now, she has more important tasks to tackle and finds herself without sufficient time to continue writing the monthly newsletter.

Serena also realizes that Thomas on her team has a writing background and is eager to take on more responsibilities. After discussing the newsletter with Thomas, they both agreed he could start writing the initial draft of the monthly newsletter. When she transfers this responsibility to him, she delegates a task she has been performing.

The purpose of delegation is twofold:

To free up your time for handling more value-add tasks and duties.

To grow and develop someone, usually a person on your team.

Both objectives are accomplished in the example of Thomas and the monthly departmental newsletter. By offloading the drafting of the newsletter, Serena has freed up time for her more important responsibilities as the department manager. And importantly, she has created an opportunity for Thomas to grow and develop his writing, project management, and other skills.

Sounds simple, right?

Unfortunately, there is much more to delegating the drafting of the newsletter to Thomas than having one conversation. At least, if Serena wants the delegation process to go right!

Thus, the purpose of this book.

If delegation were truly so simple, more managers and supervisors would be more proficient at delegating. But it is not. And that is why managers are fearful of delegating.

A common mistake and rationale for not delegating is that the manager can do the task faster and easier than anyone on the team. Undoubtedly, Serena can write the first draft of the newsletter faster and easier than Thomas. So why should she delegate something that might take him six hours when she could do it in three?

The answer: because her time is more valuable to the organization than his. This is a critical aspect to keep in mind:

Your time as a manager is more valuable than that of your direct reports. Hence, your time should be spent on higher value-added tasks and thinking than your direct reports.

Additionally, your mental prowess is valuable to your organization (that is one reason you are in a leadership position). Your cognitive proficiency is better suited for ideation, strategizing, and developing your people through feedback and coaching.

As a supervisor, manager, or leader, you wear three distinct hats:

Individual Contributor – achieving your own results.

Manager – achieving results through others.

Leader – leading people and people development.

Unfortunately, it is too easy to fall into the trap of thinking that your Individual Contributor tasks are more important than your managerial and leadership responsibilities. Especially when annual performance ratings and rankings are majorly based on the objectives and results attained by your Individual Contributor efforts.

However, your most important value-added contributions come from your managerial and leadership roles. This is why effective delegation is so important for you and your organization. Delegating allows managers and leaders to spend more time performing their managerial and leadership roles. These value-added duties are what your organization is (or should be) compensating you for.

But before you dive headlong into delegating as much of your Individual Contributor activities as possible, you must learn how to manage the delegation process from start to finish.

Delegation Comfort Level

The first place to start is understanding your current comfort level with delegation. You do this by assessing where you fall on the Discomfort-Comfort Continuum:

DISCOMFORT > > > > < < < < COMFORT

Ask yourself, on a scale of one (total discomfort) to ten (extremely comfortable), how comfortable you are, in general, with delegating your Individual Contributor tasks to those on your team.

On the far left, delegating makes you nervous, anxious, and uncomfortable. At the far right, you would gladly and willingly delegate many things (assuming you had sufficient staff resources to do so).

The ideal place to be is around seven or eight on this scale. Too far to the right and you may mistakenly delegate things too quickly and without making the proper assessments. Too far to the left and you may suffer burnout from taking on too many responsibilities and not relying enough on your team members. Plus, you will miss out on opportunities to develop your team members.

Additionally, the Discomfort-Comfort Continuum will differ for each task you consider delegating and the person to be delegated to. We will go into much greater detail on this later in the book. For now, just understand your general discomfort or comfort level with delegation.

Lastly, do not be overly concerned if your current comfort level is far to the left or near the middle. You will move along this continuum step-by-step with each delegated task and as you become familiar with managing the entire delegation process.

Benefits of Delegating

Besides achieving the two main purposes of delegating highlighted above, effective delegation has numerous other benefits for you, your team members, and your organization:

New ideas for implementation

Higher employee engagement (which usually results in lower employee attrition)

Less work is delegated to you by team members knowing you will do their jobs for them

Improved decision-making skills across the team

Improved cognitive skills across the team

Improved trust between managers and team members

That last point is a two-way street. Managers increase trust in their direct reports as these team members successfully complete delegated tasks and assignments. And team members gain greater trust in their managers when the delegation process helps them grow and develop.

Another benefit of effective delegation is that managers and their team members become clearer on Decision Rights. I will delve into this in greater detail in the chapter on *Holding the Delegation Discussions*. For now, be comforted knowing you can retain desired decision-making authority and approval when delegating.

Fears and Concerns of Delegating

There are many fears and concerns managers have about delegating, including:

- The task will take longer than doing it yourself

- Someone will purposefully screw up to make you look bad

- Not knowing how to manage the delegation process

The solution to the second point is simple: do not delegate to those you do not trust. Of course, if there are people on your team you do not trust, this begs the question of why they are on your team anyway.

Remember, there is a huge difference between not trusting someone and not having confidence in them. Even though we often say things like, "I do not trust them to complete this task in time," what we really mean is that we lack confidence in them to meet a stipulated deadline. That is different from not trusting them.

If yours is truly a confidence issue, the tips and techniques in *The Art of Effective Feedback* provide best practices for increasing the capability, competence, and confidence of team members.

As for the third point above on managing the delegation process, that is what this guidebook is all about. We will begin to grow your confidence in this area with the next chapter on *Delegating Tasks and Assignments.*

CHAPTER 2

Effective Delegation Models

Before we get into the process of effective delegation, there are four models I use that form the basis for effectively delegating. These four models are:

- The Effective Delegation Process Model
- The Delegation Assessment Model
- Readiness Assessment
- The Buy-In Continuum

The Effective Delegation Process Model

The Effective Delegation Process Model has three parts. The remainder of the book will describe how to use this model.

Part One – Assessment and Evaluation.

A. Assess the Effort/Value of each of your tasks, activities, and projects using the Effort/Value Matrix.

B. Identify your tasks, activities, projects, and assignments that could or should be delegated.

C. Evaluate the competency and capacity levels of your team members. Create a shortlist of those with the best mix of competency (skills) and capacity to handle a delegated task, project, or assignment.

D. Hold an initial discussion with each short-listed team member to confirm or change your initial assessment of their competency and current capacity.

E. Ask each short-listed team member to state their confidence (scale of 1-10) to handle the task, project, or assignment.

F. Identify additional resources each team member may require to accomplish the task, project, or assignment.

G. Decide to whom to delegate the task, project, or assignment.

Part Two – Delegation Conversation

A. Plan and prepare to hold the Delegation Conversation

B. Have the Delegation Conversation and explain the nature and scope of the task or project to be delegated, including:

    a. The vision, context, and why of the task or project.

    b. The desired objectives or results.

    c. Specifics on everything that needs to be done to accomplish the task or project.

    d. Describe how you do what needs to be done (as an example of how to approach the task or project).

C. Describe the Clear Line of Value that the team member brings to the task, project, or assignment.

D. Discuss how progress will be monitored and measured.

E. Review and discuss the initial Decision Rights for the task, project, or assignment.

F. Check for clarification and comprehension of everything discussed.

G. Check for the comfort and confidence levels of the team member before concluding the conversation.

H. Follow up on the conversation with a confirmation email of the key points discussed and all action items for you and the team member (with stipulated deadlines if appropriate). Reconfirm how progress will be monitored and measured.

Part Three – Progress Monitoring and Coaching

A. Plan and prepare for each post-delegation progress monitoring meeting or discussion.

B. Hold the post-delegation progress monitoring meetings or discussions based on agreed timelines or milestones. Minimize ad hoc progress monitoring discussions as best you can.

C. Include a review of Decision Rights in every progress monitoring discussion.

D. In each progress monitoring discussion, determine areas where you can eliminate roadblocks or clear hurdles for your team member.

E. In each progress monitoring discussion, identify where the team member can benefit from your coaching and mentoring. Coach and mentor in these areas as necessary.

Delegation Assessment Model

Throughout Part One of the Effective Delegation Process Model, you will be evaluating and assessing your team members on various attributes to determine the likelihood of them successfully handling and completing a delegated task, project, or assignment. I use the model below to record these assessments:

	High	Medium	Low
Competency			
Capacity			
Confidence			
Eagerness			
Willingness			

You will likely encounter the need for trade-offs between competency and capacity. Very often, your highest-skilled team members also have the highest workloads and the lowest capacity to take on new tasks, projects, or assignments. However, the good news is that for someone with a medium ranking on competency and a high level of capacity, the delegated task could be a growth and development opportunity for them.

I recommend not giving too much weight to low confidence levels, especially for delegating for development activities. Their confidence will grow as they achieve initial success. However, confidence is an important element of success, so I include it as part of the evaluation and assessment process.

Readiness Assessment

To determine the readiness of a team member to handle a delegated task, project, or assignment successfully, rank them on a scale of 1 (not ready) to 4 (very ready) for the following categories:

> Required technical skills
>
> Time management skills
>
> Decision-making skills
>
> Required interpersonal skills
>
> Related or relevant experience
>
> Sufficient knowledge of the organization and its policies, practices, and procedures
>
> Access to the right resources
>
> Access to the right information
>
> Project management and organizing skills
>
> Self-motivation
>
> Resiliency

Even if they are not fully ready for all categories, they could still be a strong candidate for the delegated task, project, or assignment. However, they might require more hands-on monitoring, managing, and coaching for you, particularly when they first take on the delegated task, project, or assignment.

Additionally, this readiness assessment will help you determine if they are currently ready to take on the entire task or only part of it. The chart below indicates which aspects of a delegated task should be led by the team member (highlighted boxes) and which should initially be led by the manager:

Readiness 1	Readiness 2	Readiness 3	Readiness 4
Vision, Context, and Why	Vision, Context, and Why	Vision, Context, and Why	Vision, Context, and Why
Desired Objectives and Results	Desired Objectives and Results	Desired Objectives and Results	Desired Objectives and Results
What Needs to be Done	What Needs to be Done	What Needs to be Done	What Needs to be Done
How to Do What Needs to be Done	How to Do What Needs to be Done	How to Do What Needs to be Done	How to Do What Needs to be Done

Buy-In Continuum

Here is a Buy-In Continuum tool for you to measure the level of buy-in you are achieving with individuals and groups. It ranges from those aggressively opposed to a new idea, change, or a delegated assignment to those who not only accept the idea, change, or delegated assignment, but who also become advocates and proponents for the idea, change, or delegated assignment. There are seven levels or points along the Buy-In Continuum:

Aggressively Opposed

Not in agreement

Wait-and-See / Reluctant Acceptance

Neutral/WIIFM (What's In It For Me)

Willing to Try

Acceptance

Advocate

This Buy-in Continuum can be used to evaluate individuals, project teams, or even the buy-in between cross-functional departments.

A word of caution: do not attempt to move anyone more than one step along the continuum at a time. It is nearly impossible to turn a WIIFM person directly into an Advocate. Rather, work with such an on-the-fence person to first get them to the Willing-to-Try stage. After they see the program's benefits more clearly, you can coach them into Acceptance. .

The same goes for the Reluctant Acceptance participant. All the rah-rah and motivational techniques in the world will not magically turn them into an Acceptance participant. Instead, coach and mentor them to the Neutral stage first and then to the willing-to-give-it-a-try stage. Convince them to give it a try and see how things work out.

You may need to do a bit of micromanaging here. Not quite holding their hand, but staying in constant close contact to see how they are feeling and helping to fend off any situations that might cause them to slip back into reluctance mode. Yes, this takes time and the kind of tenacity needed to lead people.

Personally, I rarely try to move someone from the Acceptance level to being an Advocate. I find that those who become the best advocates are highly self-motivated and do not need prompting or encouragement from me. Their own passion and enthusiasm will bubble up without any influence or suggestions from me.

CHAPTER 3

Delegating Tasks and Assignments

When you delegate tasks, assignments, projects, duties, or anything else, you also delegate responsibility. However, you are not delegating accountability.

As the manager, your role in overseeing the outcomes and results produced by your delegated team members is crucial. They are responsible for producing the results, which is inherent in the 'delegation contract' between you and them. But, as the leader, you will remain accountable to your boss and the organization for their performance.

This is an important distinction to keep in mind at all times. It underscores the need for constant vigilance in your leadership role.

I learned this the hard way in my early thirties. At the time, I was VP of Marketing for Citibank's retail banking operations in Singapore. I delegated the launch of an international debit card to one of my brand product managers. This experience, though challenging, was a valuable lesson in the distinction between responsibility and accountability in delegation.

Normally, I would have led the launch of such a high-visibility and innovative product (this was the early 1990s, so the card was extremely innovative at the time). I led our negotiations with the third-party service provider who would accept our new debit card at ATMs in numerous markets around the world. I was sure we had a successful and fabulous new product in place. I was confident my brand manager would create a successful launch.

And she did. It was actually too successful as customer demand exceeded our ability to supply these new cards. That was an unfortunate – but acceptable – problem to have.

Not acceptable, however, was the TV commercial and print campaign she created to launch this product. These advertisements showed the new card used in Hong Kong, Tokyo, and San Francisco. Unfortunately, none of these were markets where our third-party vendor had ATMs.

She had overlooked this detail in the 50-plus page contract we had signed. My attention was elsewhere on another new product launch, so I failed to catch this error. So, while she was responsible for the mistake, I was held accountable for it (and rightfully so).

This experience taught me the value of providing sufficient leadership oversight on every project and that being busy and focused on personally leading another major product launch (an Individual Contributor activity) was not a valid excuse.

As I said, it was a lesson learned hard and painfully.

However, it caused me to create a personal checklist for better delegating in the future. Over the years, this checklist evolved into the Delegation Process Model, which I share in this book.

What to Delegate

So, what should you delegate?

Here are some suggestions:

- Low-value producing tasks

- Relatively safe tasks

- Tasks with established procedures or processes that can easily be followed

- Things with low financial risk to your budget or the organization

- Things with low or nil safety risk to people or facilities

- Things that the delegated person is ready for or nearly ready for

The first step in the delegation process is assessing your workload and identifying where each task you perform falls in the Effort/Value Matrix. Everything you do requires either low, medium, or high effort.

Every outcome or result achieved can be classified as low, medium, or high value for you, your team, your customers (internal or external), or the organization.

Here's what the Effort/Value Matrix looks like:

High Value / Low Effort	High Value / Medium Effort	High Value / High Effort
Medium Value / Low Effort	Medium Value / Medium Effort	Medium Value / High Effort
Low Value / Low Effort	Low Value / Medium Effort	Low Value / High Effort

Here a few general examples of how tasks are typically placed into the Effort/Value Matrix:

- Reading and deleting emails is a low-effort/low-value activity.

- An email that requires a response will likely be medium effort/low value or medium effort/medium value.

- A three-day training course is a high effort (lots of time and energy required) and hopefully produces high value.

- The annual performance review for team members is a high-effort and high-value or medium-value activity. With time and experience, this can become a medium-effort and high-value activity.

- Attending a weekly status meeting on a project is probably low effort (if it's only an hour long) or medium effort (60+ minutes) and is typically of medium value for most attendees.

I recommend you record your hourly activity over two weeks, assigning each activity to one of the nine Effort/Value Matrix boxes. As you analyze your daily activity, focus on which activities create the most value and which produce the least value.

For each activity, ask yourself three critical questions to determine the value produced:

1) How does the task or activity impact your personal goals and objectives?

2) How does the task or activity impact the goals and objectives of your team?

3) How does the task or activity impact a department, business unit, or company strategy?

Here is a general guideline for future action and possible delegation:

Low Effort/Low Value	Delegate
Low Effort/Medium Value	Delegate or improve value/reduce effort
Low Effort/High Value	Keep and leverage
Medium Effort/Low Value	Delegate or improve value/reduce effort
Medium Effort/Value	Delegate or improve value/reduce effort
Medium Effort/High Value	Keep doing, improve value, or reduce effort over time
High Effort/Low Value	Stop doing (if possible), off-load, or automate
High Effort/Medium Value	Keep doing but find ways to increase value

	or reduce effort over time
High Effort/High Value	Keep, find ways to reduce effort where possible

When you have identified tasks that could be delegated, a series of questions is in order:

a) Can the task be delegated?

b) Should the task be delegated? Why?

c) What specific activities need to be performed or executed?

d) What resources are required?

e) What technical or functional skills are needed?

f) What interpersonal skills are needed?

g) How much coaching or training will be required to get someone up to speed? How long will this take?

h) Can only a portion of the project be delegated? Would doing so make sense?

Once you have identified tasks that should be delegated and understand why, the next step is evaluating who on your team is best suited to assume responsibility for each task. In doing so, you want to assess their:

➢ Competency and skill level relevant to the task or assignment

➢ Capacity for taking on additional work

➢ Confidence in handling the task or assignment

Assess each team member on:

a) the appropriate skills (both technical and interpersonal) to handle this task

b) the relevant experience or expertise

c) sufficient knowledge of the organization to work cross-functionally on this task

d) the immediate and ongoing time capacity available to complete the task within any stipulated or desired deadline

e) the willingness to take on a new assignment. Are they truly ready or just eager?

f) ability to define outcomes and determine a methodology for task accomplishment

g) the amount of coaching and mentoring needed to get up to speed

h) your confidence level in each person's decision-making capabilities as it relates to the decisions they will need to make to accomplish this task, assignment, or project

Note that these questions do not ask who is best at something. There is no ranking or comparison involved.

After you have reflected and evaluated each team member on these important questions and attributes as relevant to the specific task, assignment, or project, place them in the Delegation Assessment Matrix as per this example:

	High	Medium	Low
Competency	Ali Victoria	Sharon	
Capacity	Sharon	Victoria	Ali
Confidence	Ali Sharon	Victoria	
Eagerness	Sharon Victoria	Ali	
Willingness	Sharon	Ali Victoria	

In this example, Ali or Sharon would be your first choice. Ali has more experience and skills but does not have the capacity of Sharon. However, Sharon's skills and experience may be sufficient for the task. If the task is low to medium value, this could be a good professional development opportunity for Sharon.

On the other hand, Victoria's skill levels match Ali's. So perhaps re-prioritizing some of her work, or moving some of her tasks to another team member, would free sufficient time for her to take on this task.

This is only your initial assessment. There is a third critical factor to consider before delegating the task, which you can only determine through conversations with each short-listed team. This is their confidence level.

In the example above, you would likely want to discuss the assignment with Sharon, Ali, and Victoria first. You may include Randy and Paula if a second round of discussions is needed.

These are not the delegation discussions I will explain in a later chapter. These are initial discussions to confirm your assessment, to gauge their confidence and willingness levels, and to uncover any contributing factors you had not considered (like finding out Ali is planning on taking two weeks of vacation with his family around the time of the task deadline).

To assess each person's confidence levels, two questions are asked of each team member:

a) How comfortable are you about completing this task or assignment within the stipulated timeframe? (Scale of 1 to 10)

b) How confident are you in completing this task or assignment within the timeframe? (Scale of 1 to 10)

In asking these questions, I look for responses of 6 or 7 unless it is a relatively easy task well within their skill and capacity levels. From a very experienced person, I expect a response of 7 or 8. Anything higher would be a concern.

My concerns would be:

Are they overconfident?

Do they fully understand all the steps necessary to complete the task?

Might they be unaware of the hurdles or traps they may encounter?

The follow-up question to each response is equally important: what resources do they need to move the needle to 8 or 9? I recommend giving them time to consider this. I usually ask them to revert in 48 hours or so.

After each conversation, review your initial assessments of competency and capacity. Change and amend as necessary based on any new information or details uncovered in the discussions.

While waiting for each person to revert with their additional resources needs, you can amend and finalize your assessment of each:

Competency	Capacity	Confidence
Elevated	Elevated	Elevated
Adequate	Adequate	Adequate
Moderate	Moderate	Moderate
Little	Little	Little

Once everyone has discussed their additional resource requirements with you, it is time to decide to whom you will delegate the task or assignment. The chapter on *Holding the Delegation Conversation* covers how to handle this conversation.

Delegation Process Model

This chapter covered the key steps in Part One (Preparing to Delegate) of the Delegation Process Model:

- Assessing the Effort/Value of each of your tasks and activities

- Identifying tasks and activities that could or should be delegated

- Evaluating the Competency and Capacity levels of your team members

- Have an initial discussion with each short-listed team member to confirm or change your initial assessment evaluations of Competency and Capacity

- Uncovering the confidence levels of the short-listed team members

- Identifying additional resources team members require to accomplish the task or assignment

- Deciding on whom to delegate the task or assignment

The topic of the next chapter is how to delegate for development, which *is* the second of the two major objectives of delegating.

CHAPTER 4

Delegating for Development

T he second main objective for delegating is to grow and develop someone, usually someone on your team.

Personally, I believe developing people is your Number One responsibility as a leader. While delivering outcomes and results has an immediate benefit for the organization, developing your direct reports' skills and talents improves the organization's long-term, sustainable success.

As I counsel the leaders and managers I coach:

One of the greatest gifts a leader can give to team members is to help them find and grow their talents.

This is equally true for first-line leaders, managers, and supervisors as it is for leaders higher up in the organization.

In today's environment, leaders and managers need to take a whole-person approach to people development. This means going beyond developing only technical skills to meet job and task requirements. It means also developing your team members' cognitive, interpersonal, and personal skills.

Why? Almost every study on the root causes of the Great Resignation and Quiet Quitting trends cites a lack of development opportunities as a major contributor.

People development must become the single most important priority for all leaders. After all, if great leadership is achieving progress through the involvement and actions of others, then greater progress will be made when the people being led are constantly being developed and improved.

Additionally, people development is a highly leveraged catalyst for individuals and the organization. That is why the best leaders bring out the talents of others. Being a successful leader today is no longer about getting the most out of your employees. It is about putting the most INTO them and reaping the rewards and benefits of doing so.

Without increases in the capabilities, competencies, capacities, and confidence of your people, growth trajectories for your business unit and the overall organization will flatten. Organizational, departmental, and team results rise when the professional and personal capabilities of the human workforce continue to increase. It is that simple.

Please do not moan and make excuses like, "What if I develop and train my people, and then some of them leave?" Instead, be more concerned about what will happen if you do not develop them and they stay. How productive will your team be in that situation? How will your team results grow if your team members are not being developed to handle more complicated and challenging situations?

Lifelong learning is an economic imperative for today's times. People learn from handling delegated tasks and assignments. More importantly, people appreciate when they are growing both professionally and personally. One side benefit from whole-person development of team members through delegation: people will stay longer when they are learning life skills, not just job skills.

In addition to formal training, mentoring, coaching, and delegation are three proven methods for developing people and their talents. Of course, coaching and mentoring are automatically included in the equation when delegating for development.

What to Develop

The whole-person approach to people development, as mentioned above, includes the development of the cognitive, interpersonal, and personal skills of your team members (and yourself). This is in addition to the technical, functional, and organizational knowledge they need to develop or enhance.

Your assessment here starts with each team member's skill level and core competencies. After each individual assessment, the subsequent step is identifying projects, tasks, or assignments that will help them close gaps or enhance their current skills.

While this will vary for each team member, at a minimum, you will want to consider and include the following elements in all their individual development plans:

Functional Skills

The functional and technical skills required to perform their current jobs or next likely roles. This includes organizational knowledge; compliance, legal, and safety considerations; and organizational policies, procedures, and processes.

Cognitive Skills

Problem-Solving

Decision-Making

Interpersonal Skills

Communicating (written, oral, presentation skills)

Collaboration

Personal Skills

Emotional Intelligence

Resiliency

Growth Mindset

Continuous Learning Mindset and Skills

For each of these, and any you add, you want to help your team members grow and develop their:

Capabilities (skill levels)

Competencies (proficiencies)

Confidence

In addition, to help your team members become ready to take on additional and more challenging assignments, you will likely need to help them become more productive and efficient in handling their current workloads. First, assess their current workload levels (high, medium, or low) and their capacity to handle more difficult assignments (low, medium, or high) without dropping the ball on their current responsibilities.

For those with low or medium capacity levels for more challenging assignments, you can help them increase capacity by developing their capabilities and competencies. As they become more proficient and confident in handling their current assignments, opportunities to tackle additional and more challenging work will surface.

Delegation Preparation Steps

Because you are now looking for delegation opportunities to develop people, starting the delegation preparation process differs from that outlined in the previous chapter.

This time, you begin by assessing each team member's capability and competency levels. Then, you seek delegation opportunities that will help close identified gap areas.

You can also use this method to assign new work (not delegated work) to team members to develop them.

In crafting the development plan for each team member, determine which of these attributes do you want to increase or enhance:

- Capability
- Competency
- Confidence
- Capacity

It is unlikely all four can be developed simultaneously. Therefore, which one or two are the priority?

Then, as you think through the task or assignment to be delegated, remember that the outcome should not be just about completing the task, assignment, or project. You need to consider the outcome in terms of which skills are to be increased or enhanced.

Additionally, how will the skill increases be measured? How will you recognize their efforts in developing capability, competency, confidence, or capacity during the tenure of the assignment? You cannot wait until the end results to recognize or reward their efforts. Recognition of efforts is highly motivational and should be delivered regularly throughout the assignment.

Lastly, how will you reward them for showing measurable improvements in the selected skills being developed? Again, delegating for development is not just about the results attained but, most importantly, their skill development.

Once you have identified gap areas that need closing, the questions to ask are:

a) What types of delegated tasks will help close this gap?

b) How much coaching and mentoring will be required to help the team member handle this delegated task?

c) What are the risks associated with using this as a delegated task for development?

d) Can I allow this team member to learn from mistakes and errors, or will I need to micromanage the execution of this task so no mistakes are made?

e) Which of the specific activities that need to be performed or executed is this team member capable of handling independently, and which ones will I need to be closely involved with?

f) Would it be best to delegate only a portion of the project first and then additional components and activities as the team member becomes more capable, competent, and confident?

When delegating for development, coaching and mentoring become more critical than when delegating to free up your time. In fact, delegating for development may require more of your time, especially at the outset when higher levels of coaching and mentoring are likely to be required.

Delegating for development is often a case of "slowing down to speed up." At first, it requires more of your time and hands-on involvement. But, as the team member improves their capability, competency, and confidence, you will be able to step back a bit and be less hands-on.

However, remember that the main purpose of delegating for development is to grow and develop the team member. Freeing up your time is not the priority here. Developing the team member is.

When you use this process to assign work (a non-delegated task), you have two choices regarding mentoring and coaching. You can handle the mentoring and coaching yourself. When doing so, be very clear about the implication of this on your time capacity and other responsibilities.

Or, you can appoint a senior or highly experienced team members as the mentor and coach. This creates an opportunity for them to practice or develop their coaching and mentoring skills. So, in effect, it is a two-for-one development opportunity. Of course, before going down this route, you must be mindful of the implications of this on the senior team member's work and time capacity.

Another benefit of delegating for development is it allows you to assess your team member's decision-making skills. You also get to observe their self-confidence in making decisions, or lack thereof, if they keep coming to you for approval or for you to make the decisions.

This provides a great opportunity for real-time Reinforcing or Enhancement Feedback as needed. See the *Art of Effective Feedback* book in this series for important tips and techniques for sharing effective feedback.

As you can see, the preparation stage of the Delegation Process Model differs slightly, whether you are Delegating Tasks and Assignments or Delegating for Development. As you will see in the next chapter, there are also slight differences when you are holding the delegation discussion.

CHAPTER 5

Holding the Delegation Discussion

The second part of the Delegation Process Model is to hold the delegation conversation.

The delegation conversation may occur over two to three discussions, which turns this into a true two-way dialogue and not a tick-box, one-time activity. This builds trust and shows you are listening to your team members.

There are three core elements to discuss in the delegation conversation:

- The nature and scope of the task or project to be delegated
- How progress will be monitored and measured
- Decision Rights

For the first element – the nature and scope of the project – four crucial components need to be discussed:

1) The vision, context, and why of the project or tasks
2) The desired objectives or results
3) What needs to be done to accomplish the task or project

4) How to do what needs to be done

Depending on the level of competency, capacity, and confidence of the team member, either the manager or the team member will lead the discussion on these four crucial elements. Here's a guideline for you.

Vision/Context/Why

This section should always be led by the manager. After all, this is your task or project being delegated. Thus, you know the background, context, why it is important, and how it adds value to the team, customers (internal or external), other departments, or the organization.

The manager should also describe why you have chosen this team member for the task or project. Let them know what skills they bring to the table that make you confident they will successfully complete the task or assignment. Explaining your confidence in them may help boost their self-confidence.

Additionally, if this is a stretch assignment, or you are delegating for their development, explain what new skills they can expect to learn. Also, let them know how handling the task or project will give them greater exposure in the organization and help them build their professional and personal networks. Let them know how this project will benefit them and aid their personal and professional growth. This is an important aspect of the context for the delegation.

Observe their body language as you explain the WIIFT (what's in it for them) aspects of the task or project. Which statements seem to resonate with them the most? These will produce nods of agreement, smiles, and a relaxed body posture. Other signals may include excitement in their voice, positive and forward-looking questions, and a sense of increased energy in their demeanor.

Likewise, note the statements which seem to cause concern or disagreement for them. Non-verbal clues include rigid body posture, looks of concern in their eyes, negative shaking of the head, deep sighs, clenched fists, or tightly gripping a writing instrument. Other signals may be exhausted exhales of breath, a desire to interrupt with objections, or a slouched body indicating resignation or unhappiness.

Note how this initial portion of the conversation revolves around the team member, why they are suited for the task or project, and the benefits they will derive and gain. In planning for this part of the conversation, you become prepared to describe why this is an Opportunity to Excel (OTE) for them.

The emphasis is on describing why this delegated task is an OTE. The wrong path is to enter the conversation thinking you must convince or sell them on accepting the delegated assignment or task. When team members feel they are being sold an idea, their defenses automatically arise. This results in pushback and elevated concerns.

When you have thoroughly completed all the steps in Part A of the Delegation Process Model, you should be fully convinced that you have selected the right team member for the delegated task. You also have full (or nearly full) confidence in their ability to handle the task and grow from the assignment. Lastly, you should believe that there are professional or personal benefits for the team member inherent in this project or assignment.

If you are convinced on all three of these points, you will not need to sell or attempt to convince them. You only need to describe these points confidently, clearly, and factually. The OTE benefits will then be obvious to them.

At this point, you want to segue to explaining how you believe they will create or add value to the project or task. This is another important point often overlooked by new managers and experienced leaders. It is a mistake you do not want to make.

Clear Line of Value

Knowing how they provide value is an important factor people want and need to succeed in the workplace. Team members are more fulfilled when given a chance to contribute to a team's or organization's success. Too often, however, managers and leaders do not tell employees how their efforts provide value to a team objective, a department goal, or an organizational strategy. No wonder research consistently reports employee engagement levels are abysmally low!

You want to share what I call a Clear Line of Value with team members. It is an important part of the delegation conversation. I would also suggest it is something that should be communicated for all work activities, not just delegated tasks, as part of the ongoing effective feedback process (see *The Art of Effective Feedback* in this series on how and why).

The way to entice cooperative collaboration is by ensuring every individual contributor on your team knows and understands the value contribution they provide. This goes much deeper than being told they are "an important team member" or a "valued contributor."

Rather, leaders, managers, and supervisors need to explain – and constantly reinforce – how each team member specifically adds value to a project, the team, a department goal, or an organizational strategy.

Everyone should understand the Clear Line of Value they are providing. Otherwise, tasks become busy work and jobs are viewed as personally unsatisfying. The result is that personal motivation and collaboration decrease as little value is perceived when cooperating with other team members.

Hence, explain the value you believe the team member will contribute when delegating a task or project. Also, ask them what value they believe they can bring or create by executing the project. These may include insights based on their experience, new ideas on execution, or leveraging their internal or external networks.

At this point, the conversation is still at the helicopter level. You are not seeking specifics from them. The purpose here is two-fold:

    a) communicating the value contributions you see the team member bringing to the task helps build their self-confidence in handling the assignment and

b) asking what value they think they can contribute helps them see and describe the positive aspects inherent in this OTE in their own words.

Knowing that the work one is doing – or is about to do – provides value is intrinsically motivating. Intrinsic motivation is much more powerful than extrinsic motivation. When you explain to people how their efforts provide value to other parts of the organization or customers, they become more fulfilled, energized, motivated, and engaged.

Managers, supervisors, and leaders should highlight the Clear Line of Value to their team members and discuss these value contributions regularly. Managers should also regularly ask, "Where did you contribute significant value last week?" Or, "What value did you contribute to that project?"

Are their responses in line with your observations? If so, reconfirm that their contributions are important and why. If not, add your thoughts and perspectives on their Clear Line of Value contributions.

When people know their work is important and adds value, their engagement and productivity levels increase. Absent this knowledge, their jobs become dull, routine, and boring. And they tune out and disengage.

Desired Outcomes

The next step of the Delegation Conversation is for the leader to explain the objectives of the task or assignment, the desired results, what success will look like, and any deadlines.

The manager should also explain the resources available to the team member for accomplishing the task. This should include budgets, additional personnel, background information, data, equipment, external resources, and time.

In addition to these details, the manager should link each point to the context and the "why" elements already covered. Why are the deadlines important? What are the implications of missed deadlines? Are there any benefits to be gained for completing the task or assignment ahead of the stipulated deadline?

This portion of the conversation defines what success looks like and why the desired results are important for the team, customers (internal or external), department, and organization.

While the leader or manager leads this portion of the delegation conversation, it should not become a monologue. Involve the team member in the conversation by asking:

a) Are the objectives and desired results clear?

b) Are there any other objectives or goals the team member wants to add?

c) Does the deadline seem reasonable and achievable?

d) What other resources might the team member need to accomplish the task or assignment within the specified deadline?

If this is a Delegation for Development assignment, the manager should also explain the skills areas for development the team member should focus on and how the manager (or others) will provide support.

What Needs to be Done

After asking the above clarifying questions, the managers should now explain – in detail – all the steps and action items required for the task or assignment to be successfully completed.

Since this is a delegated task, the manager should itemize every step or action they take in performing the task. This may seem like overkill or micromanaging, but you want the team member to understand all the intricacies of the assignment. Plus, you do not want them going astray by missing a step.

For instance, in the department newsletter project for Thomas described earlier, these steps would include:

a) Developing a list of topics for each newsletter

b) Finalizing the topic list with the manager (Serena)

c) Interviewing colleagues for each topic

d) Writing the first draft of each article

e) Submitting article drafts to Serena for review

f) Meeting with Serena to discuss text changes

g) Completing the final draft of each article

h) Identifying photos and graphic elements to accompany each article

i) Submitting final articles, photos, and graphic elements to the graphic artist for layout production

j) Reviewing the final layout with Serena

k) Amending the layout if necessary and any other text/graphic changes

l) Obtaining final approval and sign-off from Serena

m) Preparing the newsletter for electronic distribution

n) Sending the newsletter to intended recipients

Note that the manager includes the necessary review and approval steps in this checklist. The manager should identify all these steps in the process before the delegation discussion occurs.

Again, the manager needs to ensure that the team member is clear on what needs to be done. At a minimum, ask these two questions:

1) Is the team member clear about each step in the process? If not, which ones need clarifying?

2) Does the team member have any questions about any of the steps? (If they ask about timing, let them know that will be covered in the next phase of the delegation conversation.)

How to Do What Needs to be Done

Depending on the skills and experience of the team member, either the manager or the team member can lead this portion of the Delegation Conversation. To build confidence and gain higher buy-in, I tend to let the team member go first by asking:

How would you approach and handle
each of these steps I have just outlined?

Doing so provides me additional insights into their knowledge and understanding of the task, assignment, or project.

After hearing them out, I then explain how I have approached and handled some or all of the steps. Typically, I will not cover the steps for which they have identified a good or appropriate approach in response to the question above.

The purpose here is not for the manager to tell the team member how to handle each step. Unless, of course, there is a set procedure or process that must be followed, such as a laboratory or manufacturing process or for safety and quality assurance reasons.

You do not necessarily want the team member to execute the task or assignment your way. You may tell them how you accomplish the task, but only as an example of what works for you. You will gain higher buy-in from the team member if they determine how they want to perform and execute the assignment.

For example, Serena may use a specific stock photo vendor. However, she should allow Thomas to use any stock photo agency of his choice (provided he stays within the budget). To demand which stock photo vendor to use will feel like micromanaging to Thomas and thus negatively impact his initial buy-in for the project.

The manager should also review any deadlines for each step in the process. For instance, Serena might tell Thomas that she has set the following deadlines for herself:

a) First drafts of all articles are to be completed three weeks before the publication deadline.

b) The final draft of each article is to be completed one week before the publication deadline.

c) Give the graphic artist four working days to produce the initial layout.

d) Provide the graphic artist two working days to amend the layout.

These deadlines should be explained to Thomas as Serena's preferred methodology based on her other work responsibilities. Again, Thomas should create his own project timeline for Serena to review.

How Progress Will Be Monitored and Reviewed

It is best to schedule the progress review and coaching sessions with the team member in advance based on either or both of the following criteria:

1) When certain milestones are attained

2) On a regular calendar basis, such as every Thursday morning at 10:30

Using the newsletter example, the review milestones are when:

a) The list of topics has been developed

b) The manager (Serena) has reviewed the first draft of all articles

c) The final layout is ready for review

Establishing the progress review dates in advance serves two purposes:

1. Both the team member and the manager know when each review session will occur.

2. The team member is not caught unaware or unprepared by ad hoc status review requests from the manager.

This last point is extremely pertinent and important. When managers call out of the blue for a status update, this is unfair to the team member. After all, your team members are working on multiple tasks and projects. So, when you unexpectedly call them or show up at their desks without warning, you will likely catch them focused on other tasks and unprepared to respond adequately to the project status you want to discuss.

Again, using our newsletter example, if Serena asks Thomas for an unexpected status update, Thomas may feel that Serena is micromanaging him. Or, he may feel that Serena's confidence in him is dropping. Neither is good for Thomas's self-confidence or enthusiasm for the newsletter project.

Additionally, unexpected or ad hoc status updates often yield little more than "everything is alright" or "everything is fine" responses.

Of course, the manager may need to be more specific on the How to Do What Needs to Be Done items for a Delegation for Development Task. Since this is a development opportunity for the team member, the manager may need to set tight boundaries, especially on the most critical steps, to keep the team member from going too far off course.

It is important that the manager set their team members up for success, especially on stretch assignments and Delegation for Development tasks. While learning from mistakes and errors is good, not everything needs to be learned from failures and setbacks!

Hence, managers and leaders should hold more frequent progress monitoring and review meetings with their team members on Delegation for Development tasks. As confidence and competency increase during the assignment or project, such progress review sessions may become less frequent or shorter in duration.

As always, it is a best practice to check with the team member on their understanding and comfort level regarding these progress review sessions by asking:

a) Is the timing of the progress review sessions clear?

b) How comfortable are you with the progress review plan? (Scale of 1-10)

c) Anything you would like to add or ask?

Now, you are ready to discuss the all-important Decision Rights aspect of the delegated task.

Decision Rights

An often overlooked component of effective delegation is the discussion and agreement on Decision Rights. This Decision Rights Model should be used for all delegated and non-delegated assigned tasks, projects, and duties. In this model, every decision a task, assignment, or project requires falls into one of three buckets:

> You Decisions – those decisions the team member is explicitly empowered to make.

> Me Decisions – those decisions which the leader or manager reserves for themselves. The team member must come to the manager for a decision or approval for these decisions.

> We Decisions – the decisions that the manager and the team member will discuss, analyze, evaluate, and then jointly decide. If they cannot agree on a course of action, the manager will decide or empower the team member to do so.

Overlooking the Decision Rights discussion is one of the key mistakes that result in ineffective delegation. If the team member is unsure of their decision-making authority, they may pass too many decisions to the manager. Doing so frustrates the manager and lowers their confidence in the team member. It may also result in unnecessary supervision or micromanaging, thus further lowering the team member's self-confidence.

On the other hand, an overly confident team member may unilaterally make decisions that the manager wants to be involved in or make. Again, this frustrates the manager and lowers their confidence in the team member. It also usually results in unnecessary supervision, more status review sessions, and greater oversight of the team member.

Here is an example of the Decision Rights model in action. As the Vice President of Marketing for Citibank's retail banking operations in Singapore, I assigned creating and launching a brand promotion campaign to one of my product managers. Here is how I laid out the Decision Rights for this project:

> You Decisions (the Product Manager was empowered to make these decisions)

- Allocation of the $600,000 budget across a TV commercial, product brochure, in-branch marketing, collateral materials, PR

- Choice of which of our three approved advertising agencies to use

- Venue for the launch event

- Catering for the launch event

- Location sites for the TV commercial filming

> Me Decisions (the decisions I felt I should retain)

- Selection of the photographer for the photo shoot (I had more knowledge of the photographers in Singapore and knew which one would not screw us on price)

- Approval for any expenditure above $630,000 (this gave her a 5% leeway on the budget but kept my overall budget under my control)

- Final approval of all collateral materials, newspaper ads, and the TV commercial

> We Decisions (decisions we would discuss and make together)

- Selection of the models to be used in the campaign (this allowed me to observe and assess her decision-making skills while allowing me to ensure that the models fit our Citibank brand image)

- The TV commercial storyboard (giving her and the agency creative flexibility while allowing me to have some creative input and final approval of the commercial concept before major expenditures began)

Not all the required decisions can be anticipated when a project is assigned or delegated. That is why, as you will see in the *Post-Delegation Progress Monitoring and Coaching* chapter, reviewing and updating the Decision Rights allocation during all review discussions is crucial.

Handling Pushback

While the Delegation Discussion process has a proven track record, not every delegation conversation will be smooth sailing. There will be times you encounter pushback from the team member. Of course, these incidents will be minimized if you go through all the steps outlined in Part A of the Effective Delegation Model and those described in this chapter on Handling the Delegation Conversation.

Pushback and objections are actually good, so do not downplay or be annoyed by them. They signal that the team member is engaged in the conversation, has some concerns, and wants to clarify one or more points.

There are two key areas in which you may encounter pushback from a team member:

a) They believe taking on the task or assignment means they will be doing your job for you.

b) They feel they are already overwhelmed with work and do not have the capacity to take on the task or assignment.

The way to handle the first objection is to re-emphasize the WIIFT (what's in it for them) benefit described at the beginning of the Delegation Conversation. How will this delegated task or project help them grow and develop? How will it set them up for a future promotion? How will their value-added contribution benefit the team, department, customers, or the organization?

And, most importantly, what are the Opportunities to Excel (OTE) for them inherent in the task, assignment, or project?

Yes, you may have covered all these points early in the conversation. But frequency is critical to effective communication. Not everything said earlier may have registered with them. Hence, the reason for the pushback. Patiently explain again as necessary.

Additionally, pushback and objections help the manager to learn what concerns or uncertainties the team member has. Better these are voiced than remain hidden within the team member and thus unknown to the manager. You cannot help team members rise above their concerns or clarify their uncertainties if you are unaware of them.

Lastly, to cover the pushback about doing your job for you, explain that the task or project is now their job. It is no longer your job. You have other, higher-value work to perform. This is not a temporary assignment you are giving to them. From now on, this task will be theirs.

It is important to make this clear to the team member. There are no "givebacks" in delegation. Once they accept the delegated task (either enthusiastically or reluctantly), they are responsible for handling and completing it.

Hence, they will not be doing your job for you. They will be doing their new job for them, the team, the department, and the organization.

As for the second kind of pushback – they are already swamped with work and do not feel they have the capacity to take on this delegated task, you have a couple of options. First, tell the team member you will gladly sit with them and review all their tasks, assignments, duties, and projects jointly.

As a prelude to this workload review conversation, ask the team member to prepare the Effort/Value Matrix analysis described earlier for each of their tasks.

In conducting the joint workload review, ask the team member what could be assigned to others to create significant capacity for them to handle the delegated assignment. This will indicate which tasks they prefer to continue working on and which ones they would like to unload.

You are not committed to agreeing to their preferences. However, for those you agree with and assign elsewhere, these become additional WIIFT benefits of taking on the delegated assignment.

As you review their Effort/Value Matrix with the team member, assign each task to one of three categories:

> STOP – items that can be stopped altogether or temporarily, as well as work that can be reassigned to others.
>
> CONTINUE – work that the team member needs to continue doing.
>
> CHANGE – tasks that could be changed in terms of frequency or deadlines. Examples are reports that could be done once a month or biweekly instead of weekly. Or meetings and calls that could be held less often.

After this review and any reallocation or stoppage of work activity, both you and the team member should feel comfortable and confident that they have sufficient workload capacity to handle the delegated task. If not, you may need to re-evaluate if the team member is best suited for this delegated assignment.

It would be best if you closed off the Delegation Discussion – with or without the joint workload review discussion – by asking the team member to self-assess the following:

> a) How comfortable they now feel in completing the task or assignment within the assigned timeframe (scale of 1-10) and
>
> b) How confident they now feel in completing the task or assignment within the agreed timeframe (scale of 1-10).

Hopefully, due to the Effective Delegation Process and the points covered in this Delegation Discussion, both ratings should be higher than previously stated.

Additionally, your comfort and confidence levels in them handling the delegated task or assignment should also be greater. If either of these is not the case, consider that a Yellow Flag warning signal as to whether or not to proceed with delegating this task to this particular team member.

While the Delegation Conversation involves many details, it usually goes quite smoothly when the process described in this chapter is followed. A subsequent chapter will provide additional guidelines and best practices for delegation.

CHAPTER 6

Post-Delegation Progress Monitoring and Coaching

The phraseology for the title of this chapter is highly intentional. For effective delegation to happen, your mindset needs to change from thinking of post-delegation discussions as "status review updates." Instead, your perspective needs to become that these conversations will be progress monitoring and coaching sessions.

A status review update has the connotation of being mostly for the benefit of the manager or leader. These check-in sessions are typically held to provide updates to the manager or leader to fulfill their managerial sensibilities. These status updates give managers and leaders a sense of being in control and on top of things. The major benefit is that the manager or leader feels prepared to answer any questions from their boss or peers on "What is happening with _____?"

While that is fine and appropriate, it creates less-than-optimal use of such status review meetings. It also means that these discussions focus on results, schedules, excuses for missed deadlines, and course correction steps. While these important topics need attention, they are only part of what needs to be discussed between the manager and team member.

When status update discussions focus only on results, results, and results, the people side of leadership is ignored and overlooked. Every in-depth conversation with the individuals you lead, especially those related to delegated assignments, is a coaching/mentoring opportunity that should not be neglected.

A mindset that you are holding status review updates causes a results-only and problems-to-be-fixed conversation focus. A mindset of having a progress monitoring and coaching discussion turns these sessions into deeper dialogues that incorporate how much the team member is growing from the delegated task, assignment, or project. It opens opportunities for managers and leaders to provide additional coaching and mentoring to the team member.

This also means the manager and team member can both benefit from the discussion. In a typical status review update session, only the manager benefits. The team member typically departs the meeting feeling relieved that the meeting is over. At best, they may leave with one or two directions on how to get a project back on track. However, these directions usually land on the "reluctant acceptance" point of the buy-in continuum.

Improving the Discussion

In a typical status review update meeting, the manager asks a series of questions (for their benefit):

How are things going?

72

Where are you on track?

What is falling behind schedule? What are you doing about it?

Are we within the budget forecast?

These are depersonalized questions, with the manager wearing the boss's hat and the team member firmly in a subordinate's role. While it is not quite a manager vs. the team member conversation, a power gap and hierarchy status delineation are definitely involved.

Again, these are all valid questions and concerns from a managerial perspective. However, a people leader will amend these questions, dig deeper, and create a more collaborative environment for the discussion. In doing so, a people leader asks:

What is going well? Why?

What obstacles or hurdles are you facing? Why? How do you plan to overcome these? Is there an area in which I can help?

From which parts of the organization do you not receive the information or data you need? Why? How can I help you resolve this?

What questions do you have regarding the next steps in this task, assignment, or project?

What suggestions do you have regarding the task, assignment, or project? What impact do you anticipate these suggestions having? What approval or resources, if any, do you need to implement these suggestions?

Where can I help?

What are the three most important things I can do to help?

With these questions, the manager exhibits that she or he is there to be a helpful resource for the team member. The manager also demonstrates their willingness to listen and understand the context of what the team member is facing. This is learned through the "why" follow-up questions. Additionally, the manager shows they are willing to listen to new ideas and suggestions from the team member.

Such dialogues benefit both the manager and the team member. They also lead to innovation, creativity, a sense of belonging and inclusion for the team member, and an increased probability of attaining or exceeding the desired results of the delegated task, assignment, or project.

Additionally, these more optimal discussions provide opportunities for the manager or leader to re-emphasize the added-value contributions of the team member and the OTE (Opportunity to Excel) benefits of the delegated task for the team member. Remember, understanding their Clear Line of Value is a highly intrinsic motivating factor for most team members.

The "*What are the three most important things I can do to help?*" question prompts the team member to analyze, evaluate, and speculate on what is happening and not happening – and what could be happening – to propel the delegated task, assignment, or project forward. This provides deeper insight for the manager on the delegated project and is a much better approach than asking, "Anything else I need to know?" These questions also provide insight into the cognitive and decision-making skills of the team member.

Also, knowing that their manager is available to eliminate roadblocks and clear hurdles can be a huge confidence builder for team members. Even if they do not leverage this availability, knowing such support is available if needed boosts their self-confidence in successfully accomplishing the delegated task, assignment, or project.

Reviewing Decision-Making Skills and Decision Rights

The Progress Monitoring and Coaching Discussions are great opportunities for managers and leaders to assess and understand the decision-making skills of their team members.

To enable you to provide better coaching and mentoring, you want to discuss and evaluate their decision-making processes, thinking, and assessments. To do so, however, you do not want to focus only on outcomes, results, or expectations. Instead, you want to focus on the how and why aspects of their decision-making processes.

Here are some questions to help you understand the how and why of their decisions:

> *What options have you considered?*
>
> *What criteria were used to make this decision?* [Note: this is a better approach than asking, "Why did you decide that?"]
>
> *Did they consider consulting you before making this*

decision? Why or why not?

What concerns surfaced before this decision? How did they overcome these concerns?

What have they learned about their decision-making capabilities?

What have they learned about themselves as a result of making this decision? [Probe for improvement in confidence.]

As you see, these questions probe their decision-making processes, analytical behavior, and thinking. Most managers only focus on the outcomes of the decisions made. Good people development leaders focus on the how and why elements of the decision-making process so they can coach and mentor their team members to help improve any gap areas.

Areas for improvement in their decision-making process may include:

Is there a tendency for them to jump to quick conclusions and rapid decisions? Why? Would slowing down improve the decisions being made?

Is there a tendency to procrastinate and postpone decisions? Why? What is the impact or cost implications of taking too long to make decisions?

Are they considering sufficient options before making decisions, or do they have a binary approach to decision-making whereby only two options are considered?

What are the strengths of their analytical skills? Are there any gap areas?

Do they avail themselves of sufficient knowledge

resources before making decisions?

Do they rely mostly on gut instincts, or do they use a process for evaluating options? What is that process? What are the strengths and gaps of that process? Would you recommend an alternative process to them?

Do they stay within the boundaries of the Decision Rights previously discussed, or do they try to push beyond these boundaries?

Speaking of Decision Rights, the Progress Monitoring and Coaching Discussion is an opportune time to review the Decision Rights table of You Decisions, We Decisions, and Me Decisions:

Are there any changes or updates to the Decision Rights that need to be made?

If your confidence in their decision-making skills has increased, are there additional Decision Rights you want to grant?

What decisions not previously considered may need to be made as the task, assignment, or project moves forward? Which of the three boxes (You Decisions, We Decisions, Me Decisions) should these be placed into? Why? Are you and the team member in agreement on these placements?

Your Role

As you can see, as the manager, your most important role in the Progress Monitoring and Coaching Discussion is two-fold:

a) Determine areas where you can eliminate roadblocks and clear hurdles for your team member.

b) Identify where the team member can best benefit from your coaching and mentoring.

Yes, you will still use these discussions to get updated on the status of the delegated task, assignment, or project. But this now become a tertiary priority for having these discussions, with the two points above taking higher priority.

In fact, it might even be a lower priority. Because, what is also important to be updated during the Progress Monitoring and Coaching Discussion is your ongoing assessment of the team member's competency, confidence, and commitment for handling the delegated task, assignment, or project.

Plus, you want to know if any specific skill competency or their self-confidence has increased. These are the foundational results a good people leader seeks, not just task or project completion.

From your updated assessment of competency and confidence, you also want to determine if any increase in either or both has created added capacity for the team member. Are they getting more proficient on this task to the point they can take on additional work? Can the enhanced skills they developed from this task be applied to other tasks or projects?

And, most importantly, for your value-added work, can their increased competency, capacity, and confidence mean you can confidently delegate an additional task or project to them? That would be an exceedingly beneficial outcome for you resulting from an effective and successful delegation.

CHAPTER 7

Delegation Rules and Guidelines

T his chapter provides an easy reference checklist of the rules and guidelines for effective delegation. It encapsulates the key points from the previous chapters and includes a few new rules and guidelines for successful delegation.

Overall

- Delegation is a process of planning, discussing, delegating, and monitoring progress.

- There are no "givebacks" in delegation. Once a task, assignment, or project has been delegated, it becomes the team member's responsibility. Only in situations where failure is likely to have major negative consequences for the team member, your team, the department, or the organization should the manager or leader step in and tack back the task, assignment, or project.

- You delegate responsibility. You retain accountability.

- You do not need to delegate an entire task or project. It is okay (sometimes preferable) to delegate only part of a task or project. Use the 4-level Readiness Assessment tool to determine how much to delegate.

- As the team member increases competency and confidence, you can add additional tasks and responsibilities, especially for ongoing and repeated projects or assignments.

Preparation

- Use the Effort/Value-Add Matrix to determine tasks and projects you could delegate to team members.

- Evaluate each team member's competency and capacity levels to short-list the most suited team members to handle the delegated task, assignment, or project.

- Determine if this is a Delegation for Development opportunity for any of your team members.

- Meet with each short-listed team member to verify capacity levels and assess each person's interest and confidence levels.

- Check each short-listed team member's comfort and confidence levels (scale of 1-10). If lower than 6 or higher than 8, be concerned and probe for reasons.

- Ask each short-listed team member to identify additional resources they need to complete the task, assignment, or project successfully within the specified timeframe.

- Review and update competency, capacity, and confidence evaluations. Use expressed interest as a bonus score.

- Identify the various Opportunity to Excel (OTE) attributes of the task, assignment, or project for each team member. Who has the most to gain, or the most opportunity to grow, from this task, assignment, or project?

- Select the chosen team member for the delegated task, assignment, or project.

- Prepare a draft Decision Rights table. What will be the You Decisions, We Decisions, and Me Decisions?

Delegation Discussion
- The manager leads the context, vision, and purpose portion of the discussion.

- The manager should also lead the Desired Objectives or Results and the What Needs to Be Done portions of the conversation. However, both of these parts of the discussion should be dialogues, with the team member asking clarifying questions and contributing suggestions.

- Depending on the experience and skill level of the team member, either the manager or the team member can lead the How to Do What Needs to Be Done part of the conversation.

- The manager should welcome pushback questions as they provide an opportunity to overcome any objections and concerns of the team member.

- If Delegating for Development, explain to the team member how you see the delegated assignment will give them new skills and build their capability, competency, or confidence. Also, explain how the development outcomes will be monitored and measured.

- Discuss and review the Decision Rights table prepared by the manager.

- Focus on the desired outcomes and what success looks like.

- Share the steps you have used to complete the task, assignment, or project and any scheduling and deadlines you found helpful.

- Do not mandate that the team member do the tasks your way or a specific way, except for these situations:
  - ➢ Process or procedures that must be followed (especially for safety or quality reasons)
  - ➢ Boundaries for them to work within (especially decision-making and financial expenditure boundaries)
  - ➢ Any actions or decisions with legal, ethical, social impropriety, company policy, or major financial risk implications.

- Ensure clarity on when the team member should come to you for anything they cannot handle independently. Also, cover how and when ethical, legal, social impropriety, or major financial risk matters should be brought to your immediate attention.

- Schedule the Progress Monitoring and Coaching sessions based on milestones or timelines.

- Check for comfort and confidence levels of the team member (scale of 1-10). If lower than 7 (for non-development delegations) or 6 (for development delegations), be concerned and ask: "What would it take to bring your level to an 8 (non-development) or a 7 (development)?"

Progress Monitoring and Coaching

- Plan and prepare for each delegation progress meeting or discussion

- Hold the progress monitoring meeting or discussion based on agreed timelines or milestones. Minimize ad hoc progress monitoring discussions as best you can.

- Include a review of Decision Rights in every progress monitoring discussion.

- In each progress monitoring discussion, determine areas where you (as the leader) can eliminate roadblocks or clear hurdles for your team member.

- In each progress monitoring discussion, identify specific areas where the team member could benefit from your coaching and mentoring. Implement required coaching and mentoring as needed.

CHAPTER 8

It's Up To You

Delegation is important for leaders and their team members to grow. It is also vitally important to free up time for leaders and managers to focus on higher value-added work and activities.

Delegation is critical for developing and growing the people reporting to you, as well as attaining the goals and objectives for yourself, your team, and your organization. This makes delegation one of the most important tools you have as a leader. But to leverage this tool to the max, you must develop your skills in using this tool.

Through the use of the models, techniques, and best practices shared here in *The Art of Effective Delegation*, you can put all your fears about delegating to rest. You no longer have to fear the negative consequences of delegating, as you will have mitigated them.

Even better, you will free up time to tackle the more important aspects and duties of your role as a leader, including more time for developing people, strategizing, cognitive thinking, and problem-solving.

You now have a proven methodology for leading the delegation process. How you utilize the process of delegating is up to you. Here are some Golden Rules of delegation to help you:

1. You delegate responsibility but not accountability. Leaders retain accountability.

2. There are no "givebacks" in delegation. Once a task, assignment, or project has been delegated, it becomes the responsibility of the team member.

3. Sometimes, it is best initially to delegate only part of a project. Use the Readiness Assessment tool to determine how much to delegate. Add additional tasks and responsibilities as the team member gains competency and confidence.

4. Always plan and prepare the Delegation Discussion.

5. When Delegating for Development, explain to the team member how you see the delegated assignment growing their skills and building their confidence.

6. Schedule the Progress Monitoring and Coaching sessions based on milestones or timelines. Minimize ad hoc progress status updates as best you can.

7. Discuss and review Decision Rights in the Delegation Discussion and in every Progress Monitoring conversation.

Remember, effective delegation requires time, commitment, and courage. Fortunately, the reward is the continuous growth of your people, more time for you to do higher-value work and the creation of a thriving development and performance culture for your team and organization.

You will become a better leader by changing your mindset, language, and methodology for delegating to your direct reports, colleagues, and others. The results will be increased employee engagement, innovation, creativity, collaboration, loyalty, and achieving your goals and objectives.

Go forth and become the Great Leader you know you can be.

Steven Howard Quotes on Leadership

Never stop learning because life never stops teaching.

Great leaders are not afraid of mistakes or failures. They are only afraid of not learning from mistakes and failures.

Peace of mind in the workplace is not the absence of conflict but the ability to cope with it without drama or victimization.

Leadership is not a position, title, or spot on an organizational chart. Leadership is a skill to be developed, practiced, and enhanced.

It is not what happens that defines you; it is what you do next.

Don't be a prisoner of your past. Be the architect of your future.

You are your life's most important variable.

You are the only one holding you back.

Progress is less about speed and much more about direction.

When feedback is combined with forgiveness, leaders are more likely to prompt and motivate changes that result in better performance and improved behavior.

One of the greatest gifts a leader can give to team members is to help them find and grow their talents.

Continuous training of your employees, especially in the "soft skills" areas of teamwork, collaboration, and working across boundaries, is the key to scaling every part of your business.

Leaders who don't listen will eventually be surrounded by people unwilling to speak and contribute.

The true measure of team leadership is not about how many team members are working but how well they are working together.

A team is not a group of people who work together. A team is a group of people working together towards a shared outcome who trust and respect each other.

Your greatness does not need to be proven. Only exhibited.

Mistakes are an iterative part of life. Mistakes will not define who you are. Responding and recovering from mistakes do.

Wisdom is not about knowing all the answers. Wisdom is asking the right questions of the right person or people.

No one is unflawed or perfect. Flaws are charming and likable. Accept your flaws. Admit your mistakes. Doing so will not hurt you. But their denial and cover-up will.

As you move into higher leadership positions, your network is part of your net worth to your organization and your team.

Don't base your desired outcome only on income. Do some good.

Acknowledgments

I want to recognize and thank the leaders with whom I have worked whose thoughts and behaviors have influenced my thinking on leadership: April Arnzen (Micron Technology), Deirdre Ball (Reader's Digest and The Financial Times), Al Bond (Texas Instruments), Nancy Elder (formerly MasterCard, now NY Mets), Goh Geok Ling (Texas Instruments), Jonathon Gould (MasterCard), Steinar Hjelle (formerly Micron Technology, now Boise Cascade), Ron Mahoney (Texas Instruments), William Malloy (Forum Corporation), Rodrigo S. Martineli (formerly Hewlett-Packard Enterprise and Rackspace Technology, now Stefanini Group), Shisho Matsushima (TIME Magazine), David McAuliffe (TIME Magazine), Ed Morrett (Texas Instruments), Ralph Oliva (Texas Instruments), André Sekulic (MasterCard), David Smith (Citibank), Rana Talwar (Citibank), Georgette Tan (MasterCard), Todd Taylor (formerly HPE, now the University of Notre Dame), and Frank Walters (Texas Instruments).

About the Author

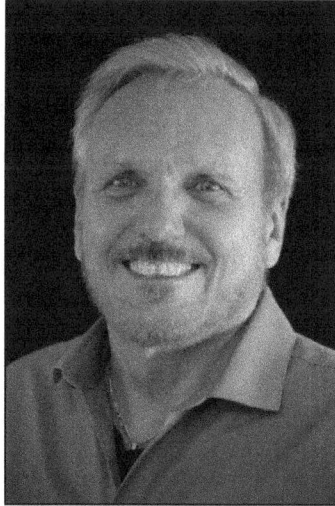

Steven Howard is an award-winning author of 25 leadership, business, marketing, and professional development books. In awarding his book *Humony Leadership: Mindsets, Skills, and Behaviors for Being a Success People-Centric Leader* a Gold Medal, the Nonfiction Authors Association called it "a significant work with an important mission."

Humony is a word created by Steven comprising Human, Humanity, and Harmony to emphasize the leading of people and the need for leaders to create workplaces of wellbeing and harmony.

His book *Better Decisions Better Thinking Better Outcomes: How to go from Mind Full to Mindful Leadership*, received a Silver Award from the Nonfiction Authors Association. He also wrote *Leadership Lessons from the Volkswagen Saga*, which won three prestigious publishing industry awards (2017 Independent Press Award, National Indie Excellence Award, and San Francisco Book Festival Award).

Steven is also the author of *Great Leadership Words of Wisdom* and co-author of *Strong Women Speak on Leadership, Success and Living Well: Lessons for Life from Strong Women Through the Ages*.

Steven was named one of the 2023 Top 200 Global Biggest Voices in Leadership in recognition of his thought-provoking and leading-edge thinking on leadership. He was also named to the 2023 CREA List of Top Influential Leaders for his thought leadership and writing.

His corporate career covered a wide variety of fields and experiences, including Regional Marketing Director for Texas Instruments Asia-Pacific, Regional Director South Asia for TIME Magazine, Global Account Director at BBDO Advertising handling an international airline account, and VP Marketing for Citibank's Consumer Banking Group.

In the past 25 years, he has mentored, coached, and trained over 12,500 leaders in Asia, Australia, Africa, Europe, Mexico, and North America.

He brings a truly international, cross-cultural perspective to his clients, having lived in the USA for over 30 years, in Singapore for 21 years, in Australia for 12 years, and in Mexico City (3 years).

Contact Details

Email: steven@CalienteLeadership.com

LinkedIn: www.linkedin.com/in/stevenbhoward

YouTube:
https://www.youtube.com/@stevenhowardonleadership

Website: www.CalienteLeadership.com

Website: www.HumonyLeadership.com

Instagram: @HumonyLeadership